BASED ON A TRUE STORY

Polly the Pack Rat

I0457293

C.M. HANSEN

Dedicated to
My Wee One, Lilipad xo

C.M.
HANSEN
BOOKS

www.cmhansenbooks.com

ACKNOWLEDGMENT

The author would like to recognize this tale occurred on the traditional, ancestral unceded territory of the Sylix Okanagan peoples.

DONATION WITH PURCHASE

Polly the pack rat was tired of being wet. She searched high, and she searched low. Everywhere did she roam! All she hoped for was a new home.

She scampered up a tree,
and what did she see?
A hidden nest of feathers,
soft as can be.

Oh-oh
POLLY, YOU BETTER FLEE
MAMA BIRD
DOES NOT LOOK HAPPY!

Into the long green grass, Polly blasts.
Deep down into a narrow hole, she went.

badger homes

Only to be greeted by someone else's scent!

Oh-oh,

POLLY, YOU BETTER FLEE PAPA BADGER DOES NOT LOOK HAPPY!

Out from the trees she shot onto the beach!
Almost out of breath, and ready for whatever was next.
She lay down to try out a newly dug pit.
Behind her, the owner was about to have a fit!

Oh-oh

POLLY, YOU BETTER FLEE

TURTLE'S MOM DOES NOT LOOK HAPPY!

Hot on her trail,
poor Polly raced for a pail!
Hidden from that cat,
she was motionless and sat.

When all was quiet, she could finally
make a home, causing no riot!
By morning time, her masterpiece was complete.
She celebrated with her pink dancing feet!

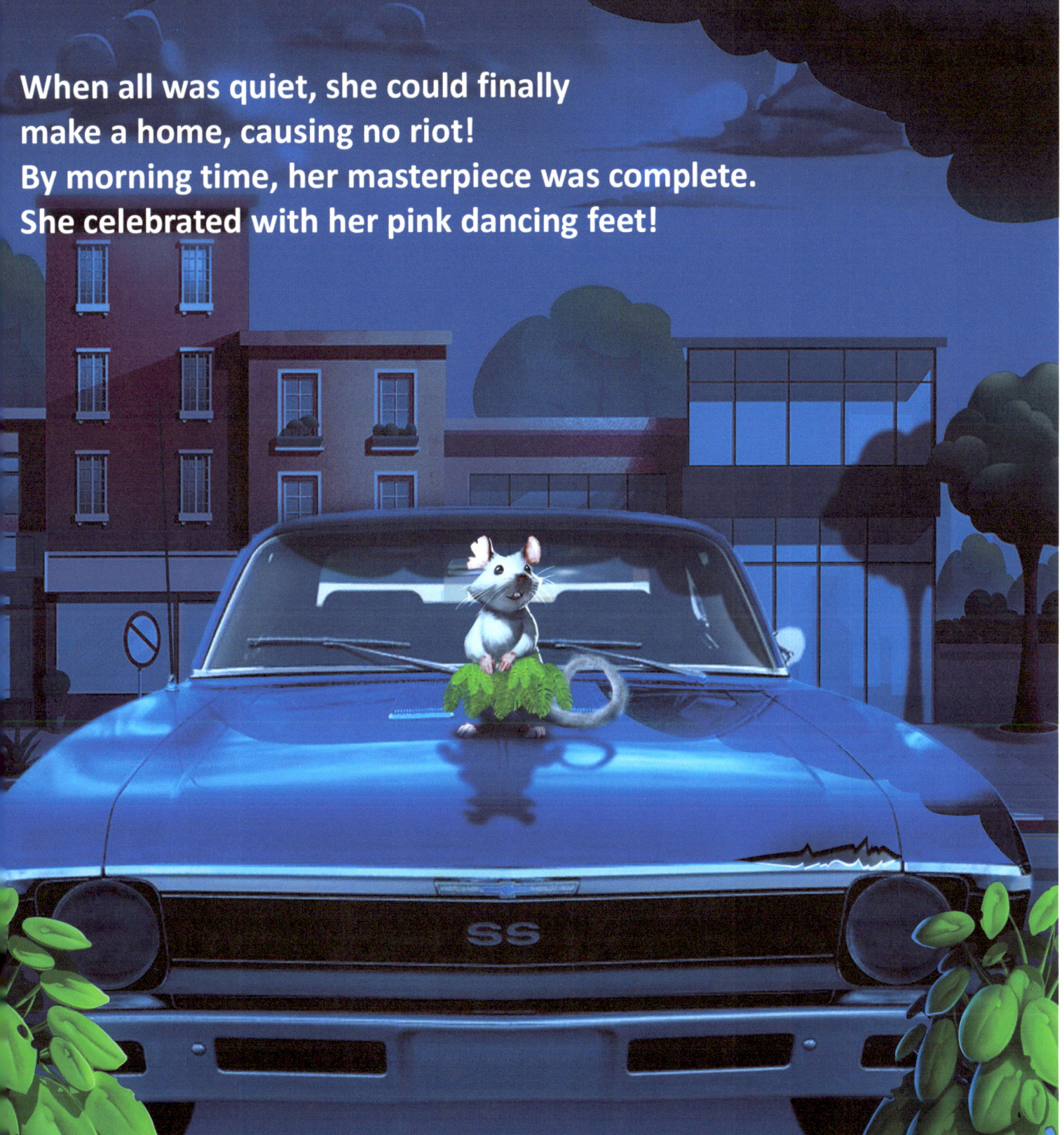

But Polly did not realize one critical thing... That rumble she heard S-T-A-R-T-E-D moving!

She held on for dear life as her home cruised along. The children above her were S-I-N-G-I-N-G a song.

Next to the bus stop, they came to a rest.
What was that smell coming from her nest?
"FIRE," yelled the Mom.
"FIRE," yelled the school kid Tom.

Everyone backed away
where it was safe from a distance,
except school Principal, who offered his assistance.
An extinguisher he used to douse the flames out!
The fire truck that came made sure
without a doubt.

Folks gawked, and they stared.
Meanwhile, Polly slinked away scared...
Resigned to the fact her luck had
D-E-F-I-N-I-T-E-L-Y gone amuck!

OHHH POLLY,
just look around and see!
Safe and sound,
you don't have to flee.

DRAW YOUR OWN
POLLY THE PACK RAT.

Hello! I am an Author and Storyteller living near Sidney, BC on Vancouver Island, Canada. The journalist in me loves to travel and collect story ideas from those I meet along the way. I am a Sailor, Mother, Wife & Senior Business Exec. Writing has always been my true passion.

www.cmhansenbooks.com

THANK YOU
FOR YOUR
SUPPORT.

If you enjoyed Polly's adventure, and want to read more entertaining tales and books, please visit my website.

~Christine